EDIFYING JUSTICE

A Wellspring of Healing

EDIFYING JUSTICE

A Wellspring of Healing
(Volume 1)

Paul Arthur Cassidy

authorHOUSE®

AuthorHouse™
1663 Liberty Drive
Bloomington, IN 47403
www.authorhouse.com
Phone: 1-800-839-8640

First published by AuthorHouse   11/22/2011

ISBN: 978-1-4678-7297-3 (sc)
ISBN: 978-1-4678-7296-6 (ebk)

Printed in the United States of America

Dedicated to my deceased father and to all who learn that they have but months to live: may a mediated right to die (MRTD) offer to you the proper and fitting end that wasn't available to him.

Dedicated also to my devout believer and altruistic atheist friends who await a conclusion to the religious war: may a MRTD propel the nations and faiths toward the war's culmination and may you enjoy the associated boost to the aggregate happiness.

Preface

How effective is the criminal judicial system (CJS) at inspiring virtuous innocence? Largely ineffective is quite likely your response based on the plain evidence that the CJS yet arms itself solely to punish aberrant behavior, not at all to reward model behavior. But what if, in tandem with its existing judicial arm, the CJS were to arm itself for outpouring ennobling justice, would you then be more inclined to concur that it will have become effectively armed for inspiring moral excellence?

As though tasked with revitalizing our nation's CJS, let's investigate the argument for our nation to create and grow—in tandem with its existing criminal judicial arm—a decidedly altruistic criminal judicial arm that dispenses ennobling justice. In this volume, we'll examine the biblical justification for such a criminal judicial arm. We'll also examine the logical justification behind each person's right to a trial deciding his life and death for non offenses generally, not just for the specific non offenses mentioned in the book. In the process, we'll examine whether the CJS has responsibility to encourage model behavior as it does to discourage aberrant behavior and we'll discuss the resulting modest change to the CJS.

We've organized this volume into a collection of essays intended mainly to broach the subject yet also to persuade readers to investigate whether the abstract concept of a balanced, two-armed CJS is worth transforming into concrete action.

Paul Arthur Cassidy

Draft110611 © Citations appreciated.

Volume 1

Table of Contents

Chapter I

Establishing a Counter-Balancing Judicial Arm

Embodying Altruism Within the Scope of Litigation

Of all the legislation that might revitalize the nation, is there really any that can compare to legislation aimed at honing the criminal judicial system's effectiveness at serving the fairer half of the scope of justice? The realm of civilness and reward supplies the nation much of its lasting enrichment; the realm of crime of punishment supplies comparatively little. Yet, scarce indeed is legislation providing the criminal judicial system (CJS) means to investigate civilness and dispense reward compared to the copious legislation providing the CJS means to investigate crime and dispense punishment. What's particularly inscrutable about the absence of legislation compelling the CJS to investigate civilness and dispense reward is that there are litigable bodies of offenses suited to this wholly altruistic aim.

One candidate we'll explore is a propitious, yet long ago rejected, category of capital offenses—violations of the first several of the Ten Commandments. This litigable body of offenses stands in direct contrast to the body of offenses ordinarily tried by judicial procedure. Unlike offenses ordinarily adjudicated, the associated mortal offenses against God alone—embracing false gods, working on the Sabbath, using the Lord's name in vain—hardly spur demands for the prescribed justice against anyone. Instead, this body of offenses offers potential to the judicial process to exhaust vengefulness and potential to indulge the fairer half of the scope of justice, yet potential that can scarcely be realized so long as these advantageous capital offenses are precluded from the body of offenses tried by judicial procedure.

Offenses that mortally offend only God directly contrast the body of offenses ordinarily tried by judicial procedure in another key way—with respect to injury claims. Specifically, while we humans are always the claimants of injuries resulting from ordinary offenses, God is the lone claimant of injuries resulting from violations of the first several of the Ten Commandments. Neither can we humans claim injuries to ourselves resulting from anyone else's violations of the first several of the Ten Commandments; nor can any person's related offenses be directly linked to the suffering of any other person. Nonetheless, we can still employ these offenses to altruistic ends, such as divulging to posterity what our generation says about God.

Based on these differences between the body of offenses ordinarily tried by judicial procedure and offenses solely against God, it's apparent that, once jurists adjudicate offenses solely against God, they'll proceed in direct contrast to how they adjudicate the mundane kind. By having omitted the need to mitigate injuries to us, they will quite undoubtedly have a sound basis from which to conduct the related trial process altruistically. As such, an increasingly benevolent courtroom would result of the related trial procedures that legislators adapt, shifting the criminal courtroom toward illuminating the fairer half of the scope of justice and away from mitigating injuries to humans generally. Correlated directly to this shift, the increasingly benevolent criminal courtroom will have become a venue for investigating civilness, specifically of the role models who call themselves to account for having committed such uniquely useful offenses.

How can we be so sure that, by adjudicating the long overlooked body of capital offenses, the CJS will manifest an increasingly civil courtroom? We can be sure because, chronologically, this body of offenses is always first among the offenses anyone commits—literally everyone commits mortal offenses solely against God from early childhood, including every jurist and legislator. Consequently, it's reasonable for us to conclude that, if ever jurists and legislators were to elect to undergo a judicial trial themselves, they would favor a trial procedure consistent with the "Golden Rule" and a trial procedure that avails the CJS of means to serve the fairer half of the scope of justice.

Litigation With Potential to Boost the Aggregate Happiness

Despite that no one other than God himself suffers any tangible injury via offenses that mortally offend only him, each generation's legislators have had sound cause to re-examine whether offenses that mortally offend only God ought to be candidates for adjudication. Merely by disrespecting the specified restitution for violations of the first several of the Ten Commandments, the legislators of every generation to date have heaped discredit on God for having so judged, thereby continuing to alienate God. On the further basis that the associated commandments head the Ten Commandments and, as such, would seem to be of paramount importance to God, each generation's legislators have had sufficient cause to honor his ruling.

By sidestepping the litigation of offenses that mortally offend solely God like their predecessors did, each subsequent generation of legislators prevents litigation from reaching its healing potential. Neither are the presumable reasons for their oversight justified: the ubiquitous commission of these specific mortal offenses by each and every one of us is hardly a justifiable reason for legislators to sidestep pursuit of the associated litigation, however repulsed they may be about hypocritically judging anyone for having committed these inescapable offenses. Hardly do legislators justifiably overlook the merits of litigation on the basis that quite literally everyone works on the Sabbath, uses the Lord's name in vain, or unwittingly embraces false gods. Nor do legislators justifiably overlook the merits of litigation on the basis that these offenses occurred chronologically early in life, virtually always before any other offense. Rather, these are reasons for legislators to realize the potential of litigation for winning victories for altruism. In this regard, some generation's legislators would well serve their generation by reaffirming that offenses against God are offenses against their nation and, therefore, that these specific mortal offenses ought to be counted among prosecuted violations of law for the good of their nation and its people.

Upon finally regarding these non-offenses as litigable, legislators will obtain vast untapped means to produce advantageous effects on society. Specifically, they can rest assured that, unlike the emotionally charged, selfishly oriented legal cases over offenses ordinarily tried by judicial procedure, any trial over violations of the first several of the Ten Commandments projects only to invoke altruistically oriented judicial decisions with potential to inspire moral excellence and to win reverence for life. That is, due to the lack of injury to anyone other than God as a result of their own violations of the first several of the Ten Commandments, legislators can rest assured that any litigation against them or anyone for their associated violations will proceed with the well-being of all in mind.

At length, some generation's legislators may find that, rather than adapting the current judicial arm to prosecute offenses that are useful for cultivating moral excellence, a separate judicial arm is needed. Based on the evidence that the current judicial arm is contrarily disposed—it is equipped solely to dispense a deprecating justice—they may further conclude a separate judicial arm is warranted. Also, because the current judicial arm rejects offenses against God as offenses against the state, they may find the establishment of a separate judicial arm is more than warranted, that it is a far preferable vehicle than the existing arm at manifesting reverence for life and at initiating the long-needed outpouring of ennobling justice. Toward these ends, by developing this prospective judicial arm, specifically its judicial procedures, they might formally ratify God's choice of capital punishment against violators of the first several of the Ten Commandments who opt to hold themselves accountable.

By so thoughtfully expanding the scope of litigation, some generation's legislators will have begun fostering the emergence of a courtroom setting absent of vindictiveness and a trial process aimed at preserving life—in essence, they will have initiated the emergence of a wholly constructive courtroom and one that complements, yet lies in direct contrast with, today's mundane criminal courtroom. They will have led the way to that very necessary social advancement in which a distinctly superior courtroom archetype emerges—the criminal courtroom fit for the trials of model citizens and, at length, the trial of God. By having created this needed converse to today's mundane criminal courtroom, they will have illuminated the fairer half of the scope of justice and, in so doing, brought more balance to the scales of justice. In turn, they will have fostered the noble spirit by which their nation may thrive quite irreproachably.

The Criminal Judicial System: A Vehicle to Virtuous Innocence?

As much as criminal acts now set the wheels of the criminal judicial system (CJS) into motion, shouldn't righteous deeds even more so? Quite inscrutably, however, the CJS customarily excludes this critical service of justice from its realm of concern with a net effect that none of its trial processes aims directly at rewarding or teaching good moral values. Yet, isn't this is an oversight? Doesn't the righteous act of instilling moral excellence belong within the realm of the CJS? Wouldn't the CJS have a much greater potential to instill social order if it were to serve justice in response to acts of civility? Let's try to unravel these puzzling mysteries.

Logically, cultivating moral excellence is a compelling goal of the CJS. How else can the CJS produce the utter defeat of vice except via a sweeping conquest of virtue? Accordingly, establishing trial processes aimed at cultivating model behavior belongs within the realm of the CJS, certainly as much as, perhaps even more than, establishing trial processes aimed at disparaging aberrant behavior. Neither can such a superior service to justice be overstated—the investigation of exemplary behavior is essential to an effective criminal trial process. Subsequent to forming the prospective judicial arm that investigates civilness and manifests praise for righteous acts, the CJS will then finally be counted among the arsenal of tools available to legislators for winning the fight for altruistic justice.

Much the same way as the existing criminal judicial arm leads prudent individuals to reject abject guilt, the prospective judicial arm will lead them to prize virtuous innocence. Similarly, where the existing judicial arm exposes the infractions of the misguided, the prospective judicial arm will reveal the good deeds of the well-advised. The prospective judicial arm will thereby tell much about its host nation—it will tell that this inanimate, yet immortal, entity is heading more toward the cultivation of virtuous innocence than it ever could via a one-armed CJS, that it is heading toward an otherwise elusive wealth of understanding about virtuous innocence.

While barred from the cultivation of virtuous innocence, however, little wonder can exist why the current CJS fails to inspire reverential awe ubiquitously. In its present one-armed form, the now extant CJS scarcely orients jurists where they may foster reverence for life. Nor does the CJS supply jurists the tools of praise and reward. Instead, the current one-armed CJS supplies jurists with the tools of disparagement and punishment. In so doing, however, it conjures notions solely of justice at its harshest, thereby reinforcing its image as an object of loathing.

Merely to provide a refreshing contrast to the dreaded mundane arm of the CJS, the prospective arm offers an attractive alternative. Beyond being a mere contrast to the existing, loathed arm of the CJS with its over-trodden path, the prospective judicial arm has ample potential to stand on its own merits. By providing a welcome path through the CJS for lauding model behavior, it has boundless potential to instill virtuous innocence. As such a life-revering arm, it will surely encourage model citizens to deepen their degree of model behavior and to draw all people to follow those role models more closely, thereby steering today's righteous nations onto a pleasingly righteous course and one that is unambiguously true. At length, the prospective judicial arm will surely become a place of praise for all noble enterprises and a place for restoring the fortunes of those whose lives now lie in ruin.

Arming the Criminal Judicial System to Serve the Full Scope of Justice

Simply by having taken responsibility to discourage aberrant behavior, the criminal judicial system (CJS) incurs an unwritten responsibility to encourage virtuous innocence by all means available to it. Beyond its unwritten responsibility, the CJS also embodies vast potential to instill virtuous innocence and potential vastly greater than any other institution. Yet, despite having an unspoken responsibility to cultivate virtuous innocence and a like responsibility to reward model behavior, the CJS inscrutably omits these vital services of justice. Neither does the CJS summon role models in the interest of honing justice at its best. Instead, the CJS trains its entire focus on investigating crime, summoning the perpetrators, and dispensing punishment. Thereby, however, it serves but half the scope of justice.

By honing its focus on the quite limited scope of justice that crime and punishment affords, the CJS fails to manifest that civility and reward for model behavior is the fairer half of the scope of justice and the more potent portion for elevating the social order. Are there not two roads through life—one of model behavior, the high road, and the other of aberrant behavior, the low road? Yet, the CJS fails the high road and imprudently neglects cultivating virtuous innocence as a result. While discouraging aberrant behavior is surely a vital function, the CJS can hardly draw attentions to the high road while so confined. Solely punishing aberrant behavior is how the CJS sheds light on the less agreeable half of justice at the expense of the fairer half of justice. To instead draw everyone's focus to the high road, the CJS needs to expand the scope of justice it serves. It needs to further arm itself—it needs to arm itself to dispense ennobling justice. Thereby, it will have armed itself to seed model behavior as never before.

Consider the breadth of the CJS's void in serving justice while in its one-armed form. Is it not to everyone's misfortune that the CJS has a void of knowledge about those who take the high road? Is it not through knowledge about those who take the high road that the CJS might begin to cultivate virtuous innocence directly? Yet, the CJS exists in a void of such knowledge. Compounding the misfortune that it unwittingly delivers by limiting its scope of justice to discouraging aberrant behavior is that it falsely absolves itself from providing an upbringing to children, thereby doubling the burden now placed on parents and educators.

So long as its scope of justice hardly extends beyond crime and punishment, the CJS risks limiting the model behavior it ought to cultivate freely. Evidence of its misplaced pursuit of justice is quite plain. With its focus entirely trained on discouraging aberrant behavior, the CJS fails to place anyone on the higher path, despite turning many away from the low path. As a result, the CJS really doesn't provide the guidance needed of it, a particularly needless shortcoming given that, as well as it serves the social order by punishing aberrant behavior, it could perfect its service of justice by praising and rewarding role models for their model behavior. Assuredly, once its scope of justice includes rewarding model behavior, the CJS will more ably provide insight to parents and guardians alike about ideal child-rearing because it will have begun examining the makeup of role models.

Creating an inroad through the CJS for role models and model citizens is sensible at so many levels. By making model citizens an object of praise for their good deeds, the CJS can and will cultivate virtuous innocence. It is how the CJS might acquire a dual-armed, symmetrical form, finally shedding light on the full scope of justice. Further, it is how the CJS might create an optimally civil exit from life. Significantly, it is how the CJS might provide an acceptable inroad through it for God to enter pleased and the only inroad where his claim, "Vengeance is mine" may ring true. So fundamental to the highest justice is legislation that creates an edifying inroad through the CJS that, without exception, all other quests for justice are subordinate.

The Costless National Catharsis

Despite having long failed the fairer half of justice, the CJS yet remains suspended in this stagnant state quite needlessly. There is, after all, an obvious lack of cost to fill the void of understanding about virtuous innocence—the resulting CJS needs only to open a path through it, a trial process, to arm itself to encourage model behavior and so fill the void of understanding about virtuous innocence. Establishing such a path through the CJS would liberate the nation rather than saddle it with costs, liberating it from ignorance about the highest ethical conduct.

Isn't moral bankruptcy poverty at its most pernicious? Doesn't surmounting moral bankruptcy thus deserve legislative attention? Yet, moral bankruptcy is perpetuated more by the CJS's continuing omission to investigate model behavior than by any other attributable cause. Neither can legislators excuse the epic disservice of the CJS for having yet to acquaint the public with its role models. Instead, legislators have cause for fitting the CJS with means to magnify the moral excellence of those role models as though it were the CJS's most crucial task. Assuredly, whether to win a victory for altruism in its epic struggle against selfishness or to win the war against poverty, legislators have cause to foster an association between the CJS and role models. Thereby, those legislators will have oriented jurists where they may truly shine—manifesting reverence for life throughout the process of investigating civilness and dispensing reward.

Justice itself demands each lasting nation undergo the necessary, thorough catharsis; justice demands each nation further the advancement of altruistic justice via its CJS. To this end, legislators have cause to consider that the advancement of altruistic justice depends on the CJS's ability to guide everyone to become a model citizen. Simply to proliferate understanding about what constitutes a noble spirit, legislators have cause to honor a mediated right to die (MRTD) via the

CJS. Thereby, they might ensure that any catharsis their nation undergoes will reap it still greater prosperity.

Once some nation finally values the CJS as a viable conduit of model behavior, the legislators of that blessed nation will have begun winning tangible victories for altruistic justice. With the CJS exalting praise for model behavior, those legislators will have begun winning their nation steadfast alliances from every quarter, including alliances with nations that scarcely trust it now. They will have conclusively shown that the current one-armed CJS is outdated for openly inviting crime and criminal behavior as well as a ceaseless barrage of cases hardly instructive about virtue. They will have conclusively shown also that instilling virtuous innocence lends to a robust CJS.

With a two-armed CJS in place, those legislators will have found the way not just to instill broad respect for the law but also to dissuade crime in the first place. They'll have demonstrated how productive to the service of justice is investigating civilness and dispensing reward as well as how counterproductive to the service of justice is solely investigating abject crime and dispensing uncivil punishment. They'll have demonstrated that a two-armed CJS is better suited as a vehicle for breeding virtue than a one-armed CJS, which quite invariably is an unintended conduit for propagating vice. Generally, whether out of reluctance to mete or administer punishment against otherwise-innocent violators of the first several of the Ten Commandments or out of an introspective admission to having committed the same offenses, they'll serve justice humbly, acculturate the face of punishment accordingly, and all without being overburdened by the costs of their effort.

Diametrically Opposed Judicial Arms

On the basis that it doesn't really reward model behavior, each nation's one-armed CJS is inherently defective; hardly does any one-armed CJS shine its beacon on the fairer half of the scope of justice. Neither does any one-armed CJS examine or make an example of those who are deemed honorable by title. As a result, no existing CJS can provide instructiveness about the divergent paths through life of those who indulge model behavior and those who indulge aberrant behavior, certainly not as well as it could if it were to grow a judicial arm whose function is to dispense edifying justice.

To correct this oversight, cause exists for some nation to add the converse image of the current criminal judicial arm, while still retaining the current criminal judicial arm. Yet, why keep the current criminal judicial arm, you ask? The reason is that, logically, there are two diametrically opposed paths through life—one of virtuous innocence and the other of abject guilt—and diametrically opposed offenses warrant diametrically opposed courtrooms. By itself, this is reason enough for some nation to employ both the current criminal judicial arm and a converse image of that arm. Further cause is that, given the rich history of the current criminal judicial arm, scarcely would any nation prosper by eliminating it but by drawing from its existing procedural and investigative advances.

Still further causes exist to comprise the CJS of two distinct arms. Combined, they project to fill the void of judicial procedures aimed at inspiring a noble spirit and at boosting the aggregate happiness—voids that the CJS can never fill without diametrically opposed judicial arms. In this regard, if a nation were to create a converse image of the current criminal judicial arm, this one dispensing edifying justice, it would serve more than symbolic justice: it would serve the crowning justice, altruistic justice, and thereby do what the lone judicial arm can never do by itself—it would lead to abiding love for the host nation owing to its CJS.

While limited to a single judicial arm and one that dispenses a deprecatory justice, no CJS, whether past, present, or future, can ever present justice in its finest light, not nearly as favorable a light as a CJS can that is armed to dispense both disparaging and ennobling justice. Even if its single arm were limited to dispensing edifying justice, the eventual CJS might not present justice in its purest light. To present justice in its purest light, the eventual CJS needs to shine its beacon on the full scope of justice, favoring the fairer of the two diametrically opposed paths through life and so much so as to encourage lay people to take only the honorable path.

Already cited among the driving reasons why aspiring righteous nations need a counter-balancing judicial arm is that, by dispensing edifying justice, they will have attained the ideal complement to their current judicial arm. With such a complement to their current judicial arm, they may proceed quite unobstructed toward perfecting their righteousness, while inspiring deep reverence for the CJS that is now thoroughly absent in its one-armed form. Still another reason why aspiring righteous nations need a counter-balancing judicial arm is to further the trend by which increasingly righteous nations become increasingly true. A most pressing reason is to bring otherwise righteous nations face to face with the culminating test of religion and with a day of judgment of sorts.

Justice That Heals Injuries

Compared to their predecessors, today's nations may seem righteous. Yet, through their like CJSs, they multiply rather than heal injuries just as their predecessors did. Consequently, today's righteous nations are hardly righteous after all, irrespective of their having made token advances in the field of jurisprudence. Neither have today's nations really distinguished their righteousness as superior to that of their predecessors. Instead, today's nations remain vehicles of injurious justice, having scarcely proven true either to God or to man. As such, all nations deserve being grouped with their unrighteous predecessors.

Evidence of the void of righteousness in their midst is the poor track record even of today's righteous nations at fighting crime and vice in general. In spite of all their efforts to fight crime, today's righteous nations hardly succeed and for one very important reason—they neglect the most important weapon in their arsenal; they neglect to advance the practice of virtue. By neglecting to laud model behavior via the trial process, they can only serve justice in ways that compound injuries, hardly in ways that multiply blessings. Neither can today's righteous nations foster the practice of virtue until these very same nations arm their CJS to dispense edifying justice.

Further evidence of the void of righteousness in their midst is that every aspiring righteous nation to date has largely undergone a frustration of its efforts to act civilly, despite having invested monumentally to appear otherwise. The same result can be expected of every nation whose CJS delivers solely a deprecating justice. Only the nation that arms its CJS to deliver edifying justice can conduct itself entirely civilly because only that nation will have acquired means to present justice in a refreshingly robust light; only that nation can ever evoke the reverence of its constituents generally about the CJS's service to the fairer half of the scope of justice.

Until they discover the mutually uplifting path of justice that fosters virtue, aspiring righteous nations can hardly boast of having achieved pivotal success in the pursuit of justice. Certainly, they may still point to small successes, but theirs will remain a form of justice that traps the vulnerable in a vortex of vice. As a direct result of their glaring omission, aspiring righteous nations unwittingly breed the very insurgency that undermines their efforts to win their citizens' lifelong unwavering allegiance. They scarcely manifest that only the CJS that dispenses healing justice can inspire optimally civil behavior nor can they until they create and grow the judicial arm that projects to breed nobility into their citizens. Nor do they manifest that solely by establishing the instructive judicial arm that lauds model behavior can the community of nations truly win the fight against crime.

On channeling travel to some mutually uplifting path of justice, however, aspiring righteous nations will achieve pivotal success in the general pursuit of justice. Assuredly, unlike other attempts to pursue righteousness, nations that arm their CJS to laud model behavior can win the fight for altruistic justice as well as the fight against crime. Subsequent to this turn in the pursuit of justice, they can rest assured that, largely as a result of their wholly circumspect CJS, their constituents will be happier, more loyal, and more genuinely reverent. By how deeply their CJS then heals moral injuries, those nations will achieve pivotal success in the general pursuit of justice: they will generate within their citizens the virtuous innocence that truly righteous nations need to flourish.

The Rising Nation's Indomitable Heart

Scarcely any legislation can brighten a nation's prospects better than legislation aimed at enshrining the fairer half of the scope of justice. Assuredly, such farsighted legislation will right a nation's heart, suiting it to inspire virtuous innocence and reverence for life, even to win an epic victory for altruism. Neither may any legislation arm a nation to multiply blessings or to dispense assurances of genuinely altruistic love better than legislation that elevates the fairer half of the scope of justice over the harsher half. Instead, legislation so aimed will endow a nation with the very heart of which God spoke approvingly.

While effectively enshrining solely the harsher half of the scope of justice, however, each nation manifests an unhealthy, hard-heartedness that earns it contentiousness from all quarters. Neither can any nation take a mutually uplifting path to justice while under the spell of the harsher half of the scope of justice but only a path to justice that is far from universally embraced. Along such a dark path of justice, scarcely can any nation achieve hallmarks of righteousness nor can any have a heart that is right within it. Instead, so long as it neglects to illuminate the full scope of justice legislatively, each nation can only manifest a heart that betrays goodness itself and a heart that scarcely distinguishes it either from its rivals or from its predecessors. Worse, each nation will have cause to expect abhorrence toward the justice its CJS serves and, therefore, toward its very existence.

If only one nation would depart from the pattern of a non-altruistic, one-armed CJS and adopt an altruistic two-armed CJS, one that enshrines the full scope of justice, that advanced nation will finally manifest a heart that is in the right place and, through the prosecution of its model citizens for their relative non offenses, it will ably multiply blessings and dispense assurances of genuine love. Moreover, that civil nation will have become well suited to lead the way for all nations to serve altruistic justice via a venerated CJS, thereby correcting the glaring deficiencies of all nations past and present. It will have reconstructed its CJS to reflect that vast good comes of singling out model citizens for praise.

By finally offering formerly immune offenders a path through the CJS, some future nation's legislators will have assured their nation of entirely refreshing prospects. Moreover, by finally forming guidelines for prosecuting model citizens for certain non offenses, they will have brightened their nation's outlook by having manifested the obvious—that singling out villains for derision scarcely hones the image of virtuous innocence; only singling out model citizens for praise truly hones the image of virtuous innocence. Most important, they will finally have given everyone cause to love the justice their CJS serves and, therefore, cause to love their nation.

With their nation's immortality and inviolability at stake, legislators have cause to reinvent their CJS—now to multiply blessings and to dispense assurances of unconditional love. To right their nation's heart, legislators have cause to choose a future heading for the CJS that will be, unlike its current heading, quite universally embraced. To this end, they have cause to engage in a legislative effort unlike any other—a legislative effort aimed effectively at offering a path through the

CJS where civilness might be placed under the microscope and where the image of virtuous innocence might crystallize. Through such a legislative effort, they will undoubtedly reinvent the CJS in such a way as to distinguish their nation from all others on the basis of its truly magnanimous heart and assuring it a revered place for all posterity.

A Preferable Path Through the Criminal Judicial System

Mindful that cases under the one-armed CJS scarcely enrich or warm the heart, legislators have cause to counter that reality by establishing the antithesis to the current contentious courtroom. Not just to lighten the CJS's current caseload do they have such cause but also to manifest that the advancement of civilization hinges on conducting cases that lead to an outpouring of life-giving justice. Legislators additionally have cause to create the antithesis of the current courtroom because, given a choice, jurists and the entire court would welcome the refreshing prospect of facing an influx of aspiring model citizens rather than a seemingly endless influx of covert criminals.

Still further cause for legislators to establish the antithesis of the current courtroom is how universally ordinary citizens recoil in fear at the prospect currently of entering the criminal courtroom. On the basis of how capriciously jurists now wield life-altering power, such aversion is well-founded, given that now only the foolhardy rise in open court seeking assurances of benevolence. Such aversion is contrary to the advancement of altruistic justice, however. Only a widespread readiness to face the court may advance altruistic justice, irrespective of how amazed everyone may be that the adjudication of offenses that mortally offend solely God could have such an effect.

On finding themselves willingly drawn into the reaches of the proposed criminal courtroom and no longer recoiling in fear from the established criminal courtroom, ordinary citizens might regard this turn of events as a microcosm of the gathering for judgment that God prophesied. They might actually begin to eagerly await and attempt to hasten that gathering. Independent of now looking forward to the gathering for judgment that God prophesied, they might also regard this turn of events as a microcosm of the way justice ought to be dispensed. In essence, they will have taken a distinctly different path through the CJS from the path taken by ordinary criminals.

To correct perspectives about true justice, life-giving justice, doesn't it seem logical for legislators to open a portal through the CJS for encouraging model behavior? Marked good may occur on this inlet, where the entire court might again and again hear and record accountings not necessarily of mortal offenses committed by model citizens but accountings of their model lives. Undoubtedly, legislators have cause to explore this method of encouraging travel over the readily established, far preferable path through the CJS. The positive effects they can expect are many and include the shrewd attempts of model citizens through their accountings to open a portal through the court for future generations to see how to live respectfully.

Among the prodigious positive uses and effects of establishing the antithesis of the current courtroom setting, one that opens an avenue through the CJS for encouraging model behavior, is that it positions the community of nations for acquiring information about God. While positioning the community of nations in alliance with God where it might experience God's pleasure with them firsthand, establishing the antithesis of the current courtroom setting positions the community of nations for answering the hard question about the existence of God and for undergoing the ultimate test of religion. Another positive effect of adjudicating offenses that mortally offend solely God is that it situates the court for producing instructive rulings aimed at promoting the responsibilities of the individual to live productively. In actuality, so prodigious are the positive uses and effects of such informed adjudication that people tomorrow will likely look back and marvel at how blind people have been through the ages for not valuing the adjudication of mortal offenses against God, perhaps even the adjudication of non offenses generally, as tools for the advancement of civilization.

A Summons to a Higher Calling

The existing CJS omits any form of summons, including every form of self-summons, to people of the finest moral fiber. By making no provision to summon irreproachable people even for their own benefit, however, the existing CJS can scarcely tap into its potential to edify the world or even provide assurances about the goodness of those people who are arguably the world's finest. While barring itself from trying those luminaries for the good of all, it instead effectively limits itself to trying a parade of rogues to no end. As a result, it deprives the world of insight about virtuous innocence and moral excellence and all because its summons are yet to be altruistically motivated.

A far superior summons to the types of summons that typically bring a person before a judge are summons designed to serve altruistic justice and the nation's good, included among which are Biblically oriented summonses by God and atheistically oriented summonses to test God. Merely on face value, such elite forms of summons are sure to appeal to model citizens under the edifying arm of the future CJS. That is, such elite forms of summons imply the occurrence of a good deed, a genuine sacrifice of a role model for God and country, unlike a summons under the existing one-armed CJS, which imply the occurrence of some misdeed. In this regard, such elite forms of summons are needed just to divulge fine character again and again.

Simply to honor the wishes of the many people who feel summonsed by God or by the test of God, some CJS and the people behind it have cause to hear such pure summons. As the future venue of truly instructive trials, that blessed CJS will have finally begun characterizing its association with people of the finest character. It will have won posterity's credit for having corrected the omission of trials of model citizens from all prior CJSs and it will have won high esteem for the people behind it. It will have manifested that trying people of the finest character transforms the CJS and its host nations and faiths into unassailably venerable entities.

Consider the type of people you would prefer to have associations with—people of character, right? Just as individuals wisely associate with people of the finest character, so should the CJS and the people behind it accentuate associations with people of the finest character. Doubtlessly, both the CJS and people generally would benefit by its finding ways to pay tribute to people of the finest character. How else are its bystanders to learn about virtuous innocence and moral excellence except through people who pride themselves in integrity? Isn't the summons to virtuous innocence and moral excellence a goal worthy of the CJS?

By finally providing a form of court summons that showcases model behavior, the future CJS will have set the stage for correcting perceptions about justice. It will have begun tapping the vast potential of the targeted right to depose selfishness in favor of altruism and will have trained everyone's pursuit of justice accordingly. Thereby, it will have begun shedding enlightenment about virtuous innocence like never before. Nor can this eventuality be overstated. Solely by providing a means of self-summons to model citizens for their good can the CJS reinforce reassuring behavioral patterns, give people means to fight temptations to commit crime, and ultimately win victories for altruistic justice that have been so thoroughly lacking during the reign of the existing one-armed CJS.

Chapter II

Breaking the Cycle of Irreverent Capital Punishment

To crystallize the image of virtuous innocence

Hardly does any nation's existing CJS crystallize the image of virtuous innocence—none single out any category of offender for praise and honor; all vilify every category of offender. Consequently, each nation's existing CJS is characterized by this omission; each one fails the very image of virtuous innocence it is mandated to instill universally. Not one can yet claim the distinction of multiplying blessings, as a truly effective CJS will, since none are yet effective at cultivating moral rightness.

The realizations that each nation's existing CJS yet fails its mission and is the source of ever-compounding injuries, are crucial ones for legislators, since they write the laws underlying the CJS. Spurred single-mindedly to correct the flaw marring the CJS, they can build a CJS that multiplies blessings; they can, via an edifying criminal judicial arm, crystallize the image of virtuous innocence and cultivate moral rightness. Nor is there any reason preventing them from achieving the true end of justice but the dead weight of legislation slanted to compound injuries.

To the end that the CJS may become a universally cherished institution, legislators may determine that it needs the formerly immune category of offender to pass through it—the category of model citizen, whether aspiring or accomplished. With the category of offender that triggers admiration now finally passing through it, legislators might more readily adapt the CJS to project an increasingly purer image of virtuous innocence. Subsequently, they may begin weighing offenses generally more compassionately on realizing how offensive to reason is the CJS's current omission to project a honed image of virtuous innocence. At the last, they will wonder why the CJS had never before been fitted to celebrate people of the highest integrity.

On realizing how prudent is propagating virtuous innocence via the CJS, the legislators of participating nations might be more motivated to initiate the overdue interim of executing judgment against the formerly immune category of model citizen who so elect it. Once underway, they may observe the overdue interim will have a cleansing effect on people generally due to its rendering a truer perspective on crime itself. That is, they may observe that the open admission of mortal offenses against God triggers an abundance of like admissions and a thorough identification with those model citizens.

Think of how refreshing the prospect will be in which the once immune category of offender passes through the CJS. By rendering the highest moral fiber to critical examination, the CJS will have begun investigating civilness with the fervor it now investigates crime. Is it not intuitive that the CJS can better foster moral rightness and moral excellence by investigating both civilness and crime than it can by investigating crime alone? Assuredly, investigating civilness with pure intention will provide a refreshing change of perspective for the entire court system. At that milestone event, the CJS will surely begin unfolding cases entirely unlike those of the typical categories of offenders that now pass through it. Subsequently, the CJS might focus less on discouraging aberrant behavior and more on encouraging model behavior, making associations with people of integrity more the rule.

The Emerging Converse Image of Capital Punishment

Inarguably, the existing arm of the CJS performs a vital function—it investigates crime and dispenses punishment as a deterrent to aberrant behavior. While engaged with perpetrators of aberrant behavior, however, the existing arm can scarcely engage itself with role models. Neither can it investigate civility nor dispense reward nor any enriching form of justice while engaged solely with travelers of the low road. Consequently, in theory, the existing arm warrants a limitation to its power. Yet, in practice, the existing arm unfortunately usurps complete control over the entire CJS.

By concerning itself quite exclusively with discouraging aberrant behavior, the CJS thereby vastly omits cultivating model behavior directly. Yet, isn't neglecting to exploit its potential to encourage model behavior an oversight? Shouldn't cultivating model behavior directly be its primary objective and the intended target of discouraging aberrant behavior? It certainly seems that the CJS might serve altruistic justice better by targeting the cultivation of model behavior independent of any need to discourage aberrant behavior.

In contrast to the scarcely inviting experience offered by the existing arm of the CJS, the proposed arm promises to offer a quite thoroughly enriching experience and an experience that may never be available otherwise. While filling the need for a civil, proper, and sanctioned exit from life, the proposed arm promises to offer jurists a mutually reinforcing means to dispense justice replete with commendations about model behavior. In addition, where the existing arm dispenses scarcely appealing justice, the proposed arm promises to dispense wholly inviting justice and the regenerative justice of repairing wrongs against God alone.

Juxtaposed against the existing path through the CJS, the proposed path promises to be distinctly superior, promising even to produce polar-opposite effects on civilization. While the existing path through the CJS sets its sights on achieving a selfishly-oriented justice, the proposed path through the CJS promises to proceed from an altruistic orientation. Moreover, while the existing path through the CJS rouses the very aberrant behavior it fosters outrage toward, the proposed path projects to inspire model behavior and an accompanying appeasement of wrath. Effectively, where the existing path through the CJS compounds injuries, the proposed path promises to produce entirely salubrious results, not just the healing of injuries but also the outpouring of blessings.

Upon cultivating model behavior directly, the CJS will more successfully serve even the mundane justice of punishing and discouraging aberrant behavior. Not just to establish a civil, proper, and sanctioned exit from life do legislators have cause to foster a path for encouraging model behavior through the CJS. Instead, to give limitless occasion to the judiciary to sow the seeds of virtuous innocence and to cultivate moral excellence, legislators have compelling cause to foster a path for encouraging model behavior through the CJS. So crucial to the CJS's service of justice is cultivating model behavior that legislators have perpetual grounds to arm the CJS accordingly and, thereby, to associate it increasingly with model citizens. A victory for altruism is at stake and, hardly coincidentally, so is honor and respect for the CJS as an institution.

A Wholly Civil Face of Punishment

By establishing the trial process behind offenses that mortally offend solely God, legislators will have opened a portal for jurists to laud the actions of those who hold themselves accountable for having committed such relative non-offenses. While substantially closing the outlet to stigma through the trial process, they'll have opened a thoroughfare through which jurists might dispense primarily edification. With awareness of their own mortal offenses as a motivating incentive, they'll have given jurists impetus to manifest a wholly civil face of punishment—a remarkable, yet ironic, event considering the grim face of punishment portrayed by their counterparts during the Dark and Middle Ages.

Appropriately, today's legislators reject the hardly civil face of punishment portrayed by their counterparts during the Dark and Middle Ages, who cruelly tortured those whom they judged had sinned against God and the Roman Catholic Church. Yet, no less will tomorrow's legislators, who adjudicate offenses that mortally offend solely God, have cause to reject the less-than-civil face of punishment portrayed by the legislators of nations to date. That is, after acknowledging that a verdict of acquittal is not the polar opposite of a verdict of guilt, tomorrow's legislators might create an outlet for jurists to implant virtuous innocence as it were a becoming characteristic of all people. Thereby, they'll have created a portal to renown that is scarcely open today through any one-armed CJS and will have caused the CJS to display a wholly civil face of punishment perpetually thereafter.

Once legislators equip the CJS for cultivating virtuous innocence as well as for discouraging aberrant behavior, they'll have made the pinnacle of justice more clearly visible and readily frequented. Through a CJS comprised of two distinct arms, they'll have acquired the vital means to illuminate the preferable path through life, means that are wholly unavailable through a one-armed CJS. Moreover, they'll have acquired means to point their nation to a pivotal discovery—that dispensing edification rather than solely disparagement through the CJS boosts travel along the preferred road of justice and brightens the face of punishment accordingly.

As long as such a salubrious adjudication of offenses remains outside the scope of legislation, however, jurists today can hardly bestow virtuous innocence when they mete punishment. While faced with an endless influx solely of abject criminals, jurists can scarcely manifest the persona they cherish, the persona that is true to their highest hopes and aspirations. Rather, they'll have little recourse but to follow the customary precedent of disgracing whoever is found guilty of aberrant behavior, largely because they'll remain without precedent to do otherwise. Nor can today's jurists mete punishment for a crime deserving death introspectively, not nearly as introspectively as they could if their nation's lawmakers were to legislate the adjudication of mortal offenses.

Yet, once legislators establish the trial process behind offenses that mortally offend solely God, jurists will then display a truly civil face of punishment, the lone face of punishment with potential to restore faith in the nations and in mankind, if not faith in God and the church universal. Assuredly, once the CJS gains an influx of role models, jurists will at last serve the justice that is true to their highest hopes and aspirations. Neither may anything please jurists more than finally facing those who inspire reverence for life. Nor may the CJS enjoy any finer moment than the day when the righteous finally begin passing through its doors.

Punishment at Its Most Remedial

Mindful of their predecessors' history of having fostered forms of capital punishment replete with disgrace and revulsion, legislators today have cause to reverse course with regard to those who elect to bring themselves to account over offenses against God alone. Namely, for all who elect to bring themselves to account over this unique category of offense, legislators today have cause to foster a more civil form of capital punishment than their predecessors ever manifest before. For their own sake as well as for the sake of those who elect to bring themselves to account in God's name, legislators today have cause to foster a form of capital punishment that directly opposes the existing form.

Upon enlisting a form of capital punishment that is replete with honor and dignity, one that is a converse image of the current form, future legislators will have in effect formed two radically different paths through the CJS. On one path, they'll have fostered a lauding of model citizens who elect to bring themselves to account over offenses against God alone; on the other, they may preserve today's handling of justice as a further deterrent to the proliferation of vice. The net result of their having formed two paths through the CJS is that they will have molded it to differentiate a desirable form of capital punishment from the undesirable form; they will have transformed the CJS into a mechanism for cultivating model behavior as well as for deterring overt crime.

Like those perspicacious future legislators, individuals also have a vested interest in the CJS's use of punishment to cultivate model behavior as well as to deter overt crime. Individuals have cause to prefer the converse image of capital punishment for mortal offenses, generally punishment by God, to any punishment now characteristically dispensed by the CJS. In addition to regarding God's judgment of capital punishment for mortal offenses to be far less punishing than any punishment now characteristic of the CJS, they may regard his judgment to be less punishing even than expiring by natural causes. Actually, they may regard God's judgment of capital punishment for mortal offenses even to be highly rewarding, something to look forward to.

Especially when understood that the mortal offense being tried is the first offense a person commits, which likely occurred as a child, individuals may regard God's judgment of capital punishment for mortal offenses as something to look forward to. Yet, why? God's judgment of capital punishment for mortal offenses against him is something to look forward to because no civil courtroom would deal harshly with a child for having incurred such benign mortal offenses. Nor would any courtroom deal harshly with an adult who owns up to his mortal offenses against God as a child nor would any courtroom favor anyone dealing harshly with themselves. Instead, it would inspire them with optimism about a happy future for humanity.

So preferable is God's judgment of capital punishment for mortal offenses to any other judgment jurists may mete that the associated birthright is deserving of a distinctive, memorable name. In this regard, after weighing the vast social benefits that the adjudication of offenses that mortally offend solely God may achieve, individuals may be satisfied with the appellation "a mediated right to die," and the acronym MRTD, to describe the converse image of capital punishment, if only because the end-of-life option it affords is their most choice and precious God-given right.

Reverent capital punishment

While hardly anything conjures starker images than the irreverent capital punishment delivered by the nations and faiths during the Dark and Middle Ages, consider, however, the converse image of that irreverent capital punishment, an image that still includes nations and faiths acting in tandem. The resulting image is one of a truly civil exit from life where the inanimate players now display reverence toward the currently banned category of offender—noble role models who elect to exercise their right to exit life in God's name. Such a fair image may increasingly brighten the more the CJS endorses reverent capital punishment.

Even if it were to relegate irreverent capital punishment to obscurity and entirely abolish the detrimental practice of administering capital punishment contemptuously, today's CJS can hardly convey the converse image of irreverent capital punishment. Instead, its omission at serving the fairer half of the scope of justice virtually ensures that reverent capital punishment will remain a quite foreign concept to it, leaving it no means to convey an image of a truly civil exit from life. Yet, isn't this an oversight? Isn't a practice of administering capital punishment reverently how the CJS can inspire law and order? Or, does the concept of reverent capital punishment belong outside the scope of the CJS? Let's explore.

The concept of reverent capital punishment is rooted in a Biblical precedent—namely, the Biblical account of Abraham's scarcely vehement sacrifice of his beloved son, Isaac. With such an abiding love as Abraham had for Isaac, the CJS might do justice toward an equally surprising category of offender—the model citizen who yet acknowledges his offenses against God alone. Yet, why make a connection between model citizens and reverent capital punishment? The reason is that, once the CJS begins administering reverential capital punishment in God's name against model citizens who so elect it, that fortunate generation will be on a path whereby everyone might experience sublime, altruistic justice. Assuredly, the CJS will then quite surely cultivate virtuous innocence where it had never before rooted.

In contrast to Abraham's reluctant attempt at capitally punishing beloved Isaac, the CJS yet administers capital punishment largely seething with contempt. On the basis that aberrant behavior typically deserves to be punished accompanied by vehemence, the CJS may seem quite on the mark. Nonetheless, capital punishment in God's name against model citizens who so elect it demands that the CJS take the opposite tack simply because model citizens hardly rouse ire and contempt like the hateful do. Faced by an influx of such dearly beloved brethren, the CJS might favor reverent capital punishment for its promise to instill law and order quite monolithically.

So long as reverent capital punishment remains outside its scope, however, neither will the CJS face the dear brethren who will enrich it nor will it engender experiences of altruistic justice. Rather, the CJS will largely hinder such sublime experiences, including the experience of a civil exit from life. While cultivating virtuous innocence via punishment may seem to represent an unachievable calling for the CJS, given its cast-in-stone state, righteousness demands otherwise. Righteousness itself urges the CJS to enliven the concept of reverent capital punishment through all available means. Nor are such means unavailable to it. Instead, the CJS needs only to vivify the fairer half of the scope of justice, then behold the accompanying outpouring of blessings.

The Preferable Judicial Orientation

By confining the judiciary to the mediation of mundane criminal cases, existing legislation scarcely positions jurists where they might extract the precious from the worthless. Nor does the legislation behind the CJS currently arm the judiciary to mete punishment aimed at cultivating moral excellence. Instead, existing legislation effectively directs jurists to disable offenders of law and orients jurists where they may scarcely rescue anyone from the downward spiral of worthlessness.

Furthermore, via the existing legislation behind today's one-armed CJS, jurists scarcely have means to propagate virtuous innocence. Neither does existing legislation provide jurists means to usher the return to virtuous innocence of anyone whose innocence has been compromised. Nor does existing legislation provide jurists means to dissuade the loss of innocence in the first place. Instead, the existing legislation behind today's one-armed CJS is hardly distinct from the legislation of past CJSs. Neither has supplied jurists the tools necessary to propagate virtuous innocence, only penalties meant simply to disable mundane offenders and penalties entirely devoid of real hope for the constructive rehabilitation of those offenders.

Reason abounds, therefore, to legislate the overlooked category of mortal offenses. Specifically, no other offenses orient the judiciary where they might propagate virtuous innocence. No other offenses implicate everyone yet mortally offend no one—other than God—which in itself is reason to legislate this latent judgment as a means to a variety of ends. In fact, reason abounds to legislate God's judgment of capital punishment for mortal offenses as it were an unrivalled opportunity to orient the judiciary where they might restore the innocence of the many whom the CJS now consigns to worthlessness.

Logically, is it not in the realm of jurisprudence to propagate virtuous innocence? While it's unquestionably in the realm of jurisprudence to decide whether a man is guilty as charged, equally surely it's in the judicial realm to decide about acts of sacrifice, generally acts of virtuous innocence. Especially when that decision is based on a single act—as in the mundane CJS—rather than the summation of a lifetime of acts, it's in the realm of criminal judicial procedures to make such a decision. Is it any less in the realm of jurisprudence to assure an advantageous capital punishment after deciding a man is virtuously innocent who stands self-accused for his mortal offenses against God alone?

By orienting jurists in their natural orientation of reverence for life, legislation establishing a MRTD projects to supply them with means to enrich life and means to overcome the moral bankruptcy that cheapens life. Clearly, justice demands it. To so brighten the future of the CJS, cause exists for today's legislators to establish a MRTD and, thereby, create not only an execution of punishment that directly contrasts the punishment experienced by any prior generation but also an orientation for the judiciary that directly contrasts their current orientation.

Investigating Civilness Procedurally

Despite that the process of investigating civilness is not nearly as clear as the process of investigating crime, legislators can hardly cite that plain fact as a legitimate reason to abort attempts to establish the fairer trial process before conducting even a single related trial. Instead, however many questions may abound about the set of judicial procedures that legislators adapt to try confessed violators of the first several of the Ten Commandments who elect to exercise their right, they have cause to acknowledge that some things are clear about the eventual set of judicial procedures—namely, the eventual set of judicial procedures will foster an overriding ascription of innocence both toward the court and toward confessed violators of the first several of the Ten Commandments; the eventual set of judicial procedures will foster an arrangement in which the state faults not the individual and the individual faults not the state.

However reluctantly they may approach amendment of the CJS, legislators surely have greater cause to overcome their reluctance by a sense of duty to God and country, persevering to create a portal to edification through the CJS. Besides, the eventual set of enlightening judicial procedures promises to provide a refreshing contrast to the highly overworked set of judicial procedures aimed at dishonoring the offenders of other laws. Developing judicial procedures aimed at fostering travel along an increasingly noble path will open a heretofore closed channel through the CJS; it will open a channel through which edifying counsel and life-preserving justice might flow. It will establish an edifying journey through the court's summary judgment process and a way by which model citizens might more poignantly serve God and country.

As needed to the general welfare as is the existing criminal judicial arm, whose role is limited to the investigation of crime and the dispensation of punishment, the targeted judicial arm is more needed to the general welfare for its focus on investigating civility and dispensing reward. How much more needed is the question legislators must ask themselves, though only by actually instituting the targeted judicial arm may legislators ever determine the answer. Prior to that landmark achievement, however, legislators can surmise much about whether the projected CJS's role would boost or lessen the general welfare.

Considering how entirely past legislators had overlooked the chosen punishment behind mortal offenses, the legislators of any nation that now administers the related punishment can rest assured that jurists will no longer do so high-handedly. Instead, by how lightly everyone currently regards offenses that mortally offend God, relatively speaking, and by how routinely they, their children, and even entire nations now commit offenses that mortally offend solely God, today's legislators have well-founded cause to guide jurists to mete capital punishment for those specific offenses only humbly and more humbly than they had ever before meted punishment for any offense and then only the converse image of capital punishment. On that same basis, they have just cause to guide jurists to reason judgments with a new soundness, to mete wholly circumspect punishment, and, generally, not to humiliate but to edify via their rulings so as to point the way for an erring world to ascend the pinnacle of justice.

Irrespective of their content, that eventual set of judicial procedures is sure to fill the courtroom with wonder and to free it increasingly of vehemence and highhandedness. The related set of judicial procedures will position the judiciary for issuing rulings that make life more worth living and death more humane and, significantly, for issuing rulings that secure peace within their nation's borders as well as among nations that question their morality. The related set of judicial procedures will prompt the judiciary to feel an increasing sense of duty and deference to God and a declining will to mete capital punishment highhandedly—perhaps for all crimes deemed deserving of punishment. At the very least, the related set of judicial procedures will reflect that opening a portal to edification for model citizens through the judicial process and aiming punishment at perpetuating honor are concepts worth exploring further.

A More Effective Scale of Behavior

Plainly, the CJS, as currently legislated, offers no return to innocence for anyone who commits mundane offenses.

Instead, the CJS is complicit that the public interminably ties the offender to his offenses. Paradoxically, however, by providing offenders no satisfactory atonement, the CJS invites upon each generation untenable guilt concerning mundane violations and warps senses generally about guilt. Neither does it tell that atoning for mundane guilt repairs no mortal offense against God, nor does it win praise from any quarter. Nor can anyone expect God to relieve the related suffering. Rather, by being so off-target in the service of justice, the CJS consigns each generation to a life of needless suffering. Worse, the CJS compounds its error of providing no return to innocence for any error so long as it dismisses the realm of civilness and reward.

Barring correction of this profound flaw within the CJS, our generation can hardly expect any release of pent-up guilt. Neither will our generation see the day when the CJS brings the nations and faiths to account. Rather, ours and succeeding generations can expect the CJS to continue singling out individuals for their infractions and, therefore, to compound the guilt of today's and succeeding generations, just like generations past. Worse, neither can today's and succeeding generations scarcely anyone until some nation gains a MRTD, affirming each individual's God-given right to atone for infractions of the first several of the Ten Commandments.

Proceeding from such a stark realization, we have cause to persuade the CJS to enter the realm of civilness and reward. Yet, why persuade the CJS to facilitate atonement for the inescapable violations against God? Considering how inescapable are violations of the first several of the Ten Commandments, we are each reasonably justified to have a fair outlook about how we might answer for these violations;

we are justified to believe we can atone as well as anyone else can, no matter how guilty of other violations we may be. Armed with such a liberating realization, we can begin the process of reshaping our understanding about mortal offenses solely against God. We may grasp that atoning for those offenses offers us a high road, a road to justice at its most sublime, and a road where we may scarcely feel guilt about our related infractions.

By then taking the high road intent on atoning our related infractions, we may take the focus of justice off ourselves and place it on the cast-in-stone nations and faiths where it most belongs, encouraging those entities and the CJS to answer for their behavior and make amends for having failed the fairer half of the scope of justice. Moreover, because the responsibility for overseeing the realm of civilness and reward falls on the CJS rather than on individuals, offenses that mortally offend solely God have long deserved to be numbered among the worst violations of law. How else can the CJS mediate their model citizen's offenses for their good and their nation's good except through offenses that are benign and quite universally inescapable? The force of reason itself compels the CJS to oversee the payments for violations against altruism and civilness, if not payments for violations against God. Eventually, upon allowing people to pay for their injuries to God alone, the CJS will have thereby provided them an otherwise unavailable path for restoring their lost innocence.

In the trust the nations and faiths will eventually rectify the CJS's omission of an edifying arm and combine resources to provide a MRTD, our admissions of mortal offenses solely against God thus offer us a release of pent-up universal guilt and a release of guilt that we may achieve in no other way. While scarcely burdening us even whose guilt is now unbearable, our comprehensive scale of behavior promises to be a constant reminder to nations and faiths to stop protracting a flawed CJS and to instate the perfect two-armed CJS in its place and a reminder to individuals that, compared to the guilt of the nations and faiths for protracting a flawed CJS, anyone's individual guilt can only be secondary.

Until the immortal nations and faiths acknowledge that the culpability of the CJS in the omission to execute God's plan surpasses that of mortal individuals, guilt-prone individuals will be tethered more by the CJS's inferior standard than by any personal guilt. Just by the realization that each nation's CJS to date yet fails to crystallize or replicate the image of virtuous innocence, today's guilt-prone individuals have cause not just to feel a release of guilt but also to perpetuate a release of guilt concerning personal flaws and other violations of law. Subsequently, irrespective of how much or little guilt and remorse they actually feel over their own violations of the first several of the Ten Commandments, they will surely undergo a collective release of pent-up guilt and, with it, an equally welcome release of forgiveness.

Oversight accompanied by honor and celebration

In the light of the clergy's controlling oversight of the execution of judgment during the Dark and Middle Ages, wouldn't it prove symbolically just if today's clergy of the Roman Catholic Church were to assume a similarly conspicuous, yet now more humane, role in any future mediated right to die? Think about it. Just as a MRTD promises to orient the judiciary to champion reverence for life, a MRTD promises to position the clergy in an equally favorable orientation—a

MRTD promises to orient the clergy to champion virtuous innocence. From such a steadfast orientation, the clergy might then engage in a quite diametrically opposed role to what the Roman Catholic Church clergy assumed throughout the Dark and Middle Ages—the clergy might engage in an esteemed role of rendering life-giving altruistic justice.

Why would any nation invite the clergy of any faith to have oversight of the execution of judgment as the Roman Catholic Church had during the Dark and Middle Ages? The reason is that, to adjudicate offenses that mortally offend solely God, participation by the clergy seems essential. Actually, the role of the clergy in winning the epic struggle for altruistic justice can't be underscored enough. Nor can the role of the clergy in winning the ongoing religious war be underscored enough. With its oversight, however, the clergy can correct its error of dashing hopes during the Dark and Middle Ages, while still poignantly reminding the world that the Lord saves his anointed.

Besides, hardly does the clergy stand alone as an injurious entity. Instead, via their CJSs, all nations to date compound injuries. Consequently, every CJS yet to exist manifests a critical flaw—each one vastly omits means to instill virtuous innocence—and each one remains seemingly bereft of means. None in its present form can wholly fill its role as a viable conduit of model behavior. Instead, while in this state, each CJS tethers its otherwise advanced nation to a perpetually lower plateau of justice. Neither can any CJS ever dispense capital punishment to admire and honor, except via an accord with the clergy. Nor can any CJS effectively inspire rectitude and moral excellence without the clergy. In this regard, better for nations and faiths to correct their glaring deficiencies in the service to justice together than for either to attempt to do so alone or to expect their constituents to first correct theirs.

Ample cause exists, therefore, for the CJS to guide the clergy into a diametrically opposed role to that of its predecessors during the Dark and Middle Ages. By at last joining forces to celebrate and honor the individuals who undergo execution of judgment for their offenses solely against God, the CJS and today's clergy may together reverse the protracted disservice to justice of their predecessors. By so joining forces to champion a form of punishment accompanied by honor and celebration, they may together set everyone's sights on pursuing a higher form of justice, altruistic justice, and away from pursuing selfishly oriented justice.

Doubtlessly, only with considerable trepidation would nations ever revisit even the converse image of the justice that the clergy oversaw during the Dark and Middle Ages. Sadly, however, a world of suffering is the product of the nations' aversion to champion the one form of punishment that is worthy of accompaniment by honor and celebration. If only the nations would allow the clergy oversight over instances of the higher form of capital punishment, today's clergy might then manifest that its predecessors disserved God and posterity by having failed to reveal any form of punishment that may be accompanied by honor. Upon finally allowing the clergy oversight in administering voluntary capital punishment for mortal offenses against God alone, the CJS will be regarded as increasingly blameless; it will be viewed merely as the hand of God obediently, albeit reluctantly, carrying out an act of God. Moreover, its efforts to now honor and celebrate offenders against God alone would be symbolically just, considering its having historically administered capital punishment to torment all offenders.

Stemming the Rush to Judgment

While merely slowing the rush to judgment would itself be an astonishing turn in the pursuit of justice given that, today, the inveterate rush to judgment is so grossly exploited, a legislated MRTD would virtually halt the rush to judgment. Yet, why? A legislated MRTD would virtually halt the rush to judgment by shifting the focus of adjudication from punishment for aberrant behavior to reward for model behavior, thereby exhausting inclinations to bring anyone to justice for any mundane offense. Instead, with the focus of adjudication on rewarding model behavior, it will detoxify the souls of nations and individuals of such arrogant tendencies as the perverted love to mete punishment and cause the rush to judge to give way to a rush to exonerate, including a rush to exonerate God.

Once legislators establish a MRTD, thereby shifting the focus of adjudication to the reward of model behavior for everyone's good, jurists will serve justice far differently from the way prior jurists did. Reassuringly, they will have cause for feeling satisfaction about their new service to justice and a due and fuller satisfaction, unlike the empty satisfaction they likely otherwise felt about their service to justice while under a one-armed CJS. Giving them further cause for feeling satisfaction about their service to justice through adjudicating offenses that mortally offend solely God is their having produced a life-giving turn of justice, which succeeding generations of jurists may turn to with equal pride. Giving them cause still further for feeling satisfaction about their service to justice is that the adjudication of mortal offenses against God will have spawned in them a newfound humility in the adjudication of mundane offenses.

Until legislators shift the focus of adjudication from investigating crime to investigating civilness, however, the proverbial rush to judgment can hardly dissipate. Nor can legislators stifle the rush to judgment merely by slowing further the already slow process of justice. Instead, by neglecting to shift the focus of adjudication to the investigation of model behavior, they will have done nothing to address the reason why so many rush to judgment—for the perverted love to mete tormenting punishment against people they hate. To challenge this inveterate propensity to rush to judgment even against the hateful, they have cause to adjudicate offenses that mortally offend solely God, wherein they will gain ample resources to abide the spirit of forgiveness and tame the otherwise mutually destructive, urge to rush to judgment.

After legislators establish a MRTD, therefore, even highly judgmental individuals might find themselves equating violations of the first several of the Ten Commandments increasingly with the worst crimes that may be committed against humanity. Biblically, they would be justified to do so given that mortal offenders were to receive the same punishment as murderers, adulterers, sexual deviants, etc. []. They may even acknowledge that publicly acknowledging mortal offenses is far better than publicly acknowledging any other sin deserving of death. They may finally realize that equating mortal offenses against God alone with the worst crimes that may be committed in effect shields them from incrimination for crimes traditionally held as worst of all and buys them a mantle of religious purity, which conceals that they may question their faith, sin against their faith, and generally devote faith little power over their lives.

Yet, most of all, even highly judgmental individuals might find themselves equating sins against the Sabbath with the worst crimes that may be committed simply to steer their nation toward its day of judgment.

While halting the rush to judgment of neighbor against neighbor, the turn of justice toward edification via the adjudication of offenses that mortally offend solely God will quite undoubtedly produce a rush to exonerate neighbor by neighbor. Accordingly, if only forgiving nations and individuals gave consideration to the targeted right, they might begin to weigh even the worst sinner's avowed intent to exercise the targeted right in his favor, perhaps so completely as to count him pure. They might begin generating cause for hope in the targeted right and such a real hope as to produce manifest fulfillment of the biblical prophecy, " . . . though your sins be scarlet, they shall be as white as snow [cf. Isaiah 1:18]." Subsequently, they may regard this hope for a cleansing, purgative effect via the targeted right as increasingly realistic despite that it is now maligned by disuse and despite that scarcely has a movement surfaced in the public arena to give the targeted right the examination it warrants.

The Unfairly Disparaged Title

How extensive is our void of virtuous innocence! How deep is our need to fill that void! Case in point—not reverential awe but empty tradition compels lay individuals to address jurists and legislators by the title "Honorable," does it not? Worse, until those deemed honorable by title hone the CJS's effectiveness at filling our void of virtuous innocence, lay individuals can scarcely resist succumbing to the temptation to hold jurists and legislators in dubious regard who, on the one hand, appear above reproach but who, on the other hand, sidestep the punishment for offenses that mortally offend solely God.

Despite that empty tradition now compels individuals to address jurists and legislators by the title "Honorable," hardly are individual jurists and legislators to blame that their title conjures emptiness rather than a concrete understanding of what makes those who bear it honorable beyond the ordinary citizen. Neither are they to blame that no public window into their virtuous innocence exists. Rather, the CJS, as currently legislated, is to blame for the void of virtuous innocence. Moreover, the reigning one-armed CJS will remain solely to blame so long as it spotlights not honorable but dishonorable people and it dispenses not edifying but disparaging justice. Nor can the CJS repair the damage to justice it causes except by finally investigating civilness and dispensing reward.

What a tragic irony it is that the CJS omits examining civilness and dispensing reward! So long as the CJS reveals no proper knowledge of the deeds of life's role models, but intimate knowledge of the misdeeds of rogues, neither jurists nor legislators will be able to serve the full scope of justice. Nor may the CJS as now configured win them reverential awe, irrespective that they may still command the title of "Honorable." Instead, the continuing omission by the CJS to investigate civility and dispense reward can only preserve today's opaque view of the civilness of these best role models, preserving also a public lack appreciation of what makes them honorable beyond the average person.

Despite how untenable is the public view of role models generally today, the void of understanding about their civilness is hardly insurmountable. Instead, jurists and legislators need only sanction a MRTD in order to fill the void of virtuous innocence. Not only will this action rectify the continuing omission by the CJS to investigate civility and dispense reward but it will also reveal them to be representative of the category of offender through whom the future two-armed CJS may best project the image of virtuous innocence. Subsequently, by the force of reason, jurists and legislators will enjoy the title "Honorable" unchallenged.

Once it sanctions a MRTD and thereby begins investigating civilness and dispensing reward, the CJS will win more than reverence for all who hold the title of "Honorable"; it will more than fill the void of virtuous innocence that plagues us all—it will hone a rigorous image of the model citizen, now with a public window into the exemplary behavior of many the CJS had no knowledge of before. At the same time, it will dispel allusions of impurity in the jurists and legislators behind the CJS. Instead, with public knowledge now of their noble character, it will further elevate their station and to the extent that anyone who now unfairly disparages them for their title will reverse course and feel genuinely thankful about how dutifully they fill their role.

Its Criminal Judicial System: Whether a Nation Becomes an Object of Reverence

Via its CJS, each nation has vast, though scarcely tapped, potential to win genuine reverence from other nations and from its own citizens—namely, by sanctioning a MRTD based on the first several of the Ten Commandments and, thereby, effectively creating an edifying judicial arm, each nation could more readily find the good in its citizens and its fellow nations. It could direct its CJS to hone the image of virtuous innocence and so join the extraordinary pursuit of justice that promises to win for each nation an unparalleled level of reverence for and support for it. So engaged, each nation might undergo potentially cathartic effects, healthful effects that it can never experience merely while directing the pursuit of justice toward baiting and responding to acts of abject crime.

Unfortunately, however, quite the opposite has occurred; each nation has inscrutably failed to arm its CJS to cultivate virtuous innocence. Instead, each nation has armed its CJS for dispensing disparaging justice only, not at all for dispensing edifying justice; each nation has armed its CJS for punishing abject guilt never for rewarding virtuous innocence. In effect, by neglecting to establish an edifying judicial arm that rewards virtuous innocence, each nation deprives itself of means to achieve its system of good moral values. Compounding its error, each nation instead has honed its CJS to look for and extract worthlessness from people with the net effect of largely reaping impoverishment rather than enrichment.

Rather than make an example of model behavior, each nation's existing CJS, in effect, makes an example of aberrant behavior. Thereby, however, each nation's existing CJS disastrously hinders perceptions about justice at its best. In its present form, it subjects unwary people to irresistible temptations to commit crime. It undermines its ability to look for and bring out the good in people by omitting the category of offender most apt to provide instructiveness. In the light of its utter failure to extract the precious from the worthless, is it really any wonder why each nation's existing CJS is subjected to so much derision?

Nevertheless, each nation's existing CJS is hardly consigned to such a miserable state. Justice itself dictates that the CJS of each nation breed virtuous innocence; justice dictates that each nation correct its CJS in order that bad actors may be few and role models many. Eventually, once some nation arms its CJS more to hone model behavior than to reject aberrant behavior, it will have begun to win the undying esteem of people at home and nations abroad. It will have found in the sweeping conquest of virtue a sure way to eradicate vice as well as a sure way to propagate goodness. It will have become an object of reverence as never before for having armed its CJS with as much occasion to edify as each existing nation's CJS is now armed with occasion to punish.

On finally recognizing that the utter defeat of vice is wholly dependent on the sweeping conquest of virtue, the future two-armed CJS will surely appear regal compared to the existing one-armed CJS. It will have been devised to illustrate not only the difference between edifying and disparaging justice but also the striking dichotomy between the existing branch of the CJS and the branch it's missing. Best of all, by investigating civilness and dispensing reward with the thoroughness it now investigates crime and dispenses punishment, it will have manifested itself as the first ever CJS that provides a continual source of assurances about the goodness of its model citizens. Assuredly, once armed to purvey virtuous innocence, the CJS will not only elevate people to the pinnacle of justice but also it will deter future nations from lapsing into the dualistic justice that typifies nations today. Thereby, it will have finally been groomed into an unassailably revered institution.

Volume I

Postscript

Interested in reading future drafts of "Edifying Justice: A Wellspring of Healing" or its unreleased companion volumes? Indicate your interest preferably via e-mail: paularthur. edifyingjustice@yahoo.com or voicemail: 978-343-8437 from 7:00AM to 7PM EST.

Feel free also to indicate your interest in seeing EdifyingJustice.org become a functioning website and non profit organization under Section 501c of the Internal Revenue Code.

What might you expect in the unreleased volumes? In one, we expect to explore the keen interest atheists and non-atheists alike might develop in the associated transformation to the CJS. In the same or another unreleased volume, we expect to explore why the medically terminal likewise might develop keen interest in the associated transformation to the CJS and we expect to discuss how to garner legislative interest in the associated transformation to the CJS. In the same or still another unreleased volume, we expect to broach how we think legislators might implement the associated change to the CJS.

Bio: Paul Arthur Cassidy

As a software engineer at ZOLL Medical Corporation in Chelmsford, Mass. for the last 14 years, Paul Arthur feels very privileged to have worked alongside some of the very role models who inspired him to write this book.

Throughout his childhood, he hailed from Westford, Mass. Now 60, he lives in Fitchburg, Mass., has yet to marry, or have children.

A card-carrying member of the Thin-Ice Skating Club no longer, he recently nearly drowned during an ice-skating mishap, chillingly reminding him of the urgency to share his vision of how the CJS might more effectively serve the full scope of justice. Read the dramatic account of the daring maneuver used to rescue him and see his photograph in the November-December 2011 issue of *Yankee Magazine*.